Mommy Loves Baby

A Heartwarming Story About a Toddler
Welcoming a New Baby Sibling

Written & Designed
by
Latoya Belfon

❦

For My Son Khai, as he welcomes his new brother Khali.
Mommy Loves You Both!

ISBN: 978-1-990420-20-7

LAB WORKS
PUBLISHING

This book belongs to someone very special...

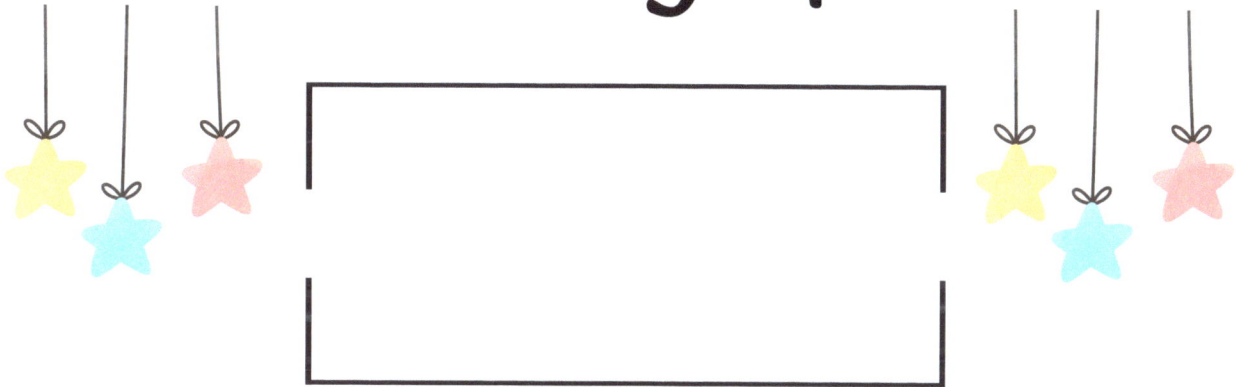

Just like in this story, love grows when families grow.
Mommy and Daddy love you so much, and they are excited to see you
become the most amazing big sibling!
May this book remind you that you are cherished, loved, and an
important part of this growing family.
Cherish every hug, giggle, and adventure together!"

The feeling of excitement ran throughout the house. Mommy and Daddy hugged. Then Daddy smiled and touched Mommy's tummy.

Confused and filled with questions, Noah went between Mommy and Daddy, hoping to receive some hugs of his own.

Mommy sang to him- "Mommy loves Baby, Mommy loves Baby, Mommy loves Baby, Mommy loves you.

The warmth of his mother's arms, her soft, soothing voice, had washed away his worry. He snuggled in closer and smiled.

Noah grabbed his favourite yellow ball the following day, hoping he could play with his dad.

His dad was holding his mom's hands and talking to her tummy.

Afraid he was missing out, Noah threw the ball on the floor and jumped between mom and dad.

Daddy sang. Daddy loves Baby,
Daddy loves Baby, Daddy loves Baby,
Daddy loves you.

After some time had passed, Noah watched his mommy's tummy GROW and GROW.

What type of ball could ever be that big? Why wouldn't mommy play with ME like she used to?

He didn't know how to ask all the questions bouncing around in his little head.

He didn't know how to ask all the questions bouncing around in his little head.

He overheard Mommy singing his song in her room but he wasn't there.
His little ears were placed on the door, and he was curiously listening in.
Who was Mommy singing his song to?

He burst through the door, eager to find out. With the sudden noise, Mommy sat up alarmed and stared at Noah. His face was filled with sadness as if to say- Is there someone else that Mommy loves?

Mommy knew -just like mothers do-
when something wasn't right with their
little ones. She reached out her arms
for him, and with a big grin, he ran into
them.

Daddy arrived just in time to explain to Noah who Mommy was singing to. Noah listened attentively as Mommy and Daddy told him he was going to be a big brother. And that meant there would be even more love in their home.

A little brother who will be his best friend forever and who would learn how to be the best son ever from him. They explained that even though they sung this song to the new baby, the love that Mommy and Daddy has for Noah will only get bigger and bigger.

Confused and filled with questions, Noah went between Mommy and Daddy, hoping to receive some hugs of his own.

Soon after, the big day had arrived. Noah was finally going to be a big brother.

As soon as he walked closer to the baby's room, he heard- Brother loves baby, brother loves baby, brother loves baby.....

With a sudden burst of joy, he ran to see
his little baby brother, he looked down at
the most beautiful sight, and said....

BROTHER LOVES YOU!

Get Ready to Welcome Your New Baby!

Here are five special things you can do to be an amazing big brother or sister!

⭐ **Sing a Sweet Song**
Babies love hearing your voice! Try singing them a little song or talking to them softly.

⭐ **Help Mommy & Daddy**
You can be a great helper! Bring a diaper, a blanket, or even just give a big smile to make baby happy.

⭐ **Show Gentle Hands**
Babies are tiny! Practice touching them gently, just like petting a soft stuffed animal.

⭐ **Share a Story**
You can read a book to your baby, just like Mommy reads to you! Even showing pictures helps baby learn.

⭐ **Give Lots of Love**
Your hugs, kisses, and snuggles make baby feel safe and loved—because you are the best big sibling ever!

❤️ Mommy and Daddy are so proud of you! Baby is lucky to have YOU as their big sibling!

Visit Our Youtube Channel

Watch & Enjoy More Stories on Story Land Playground!

Love The Lion Cub's Big Adventure? The fun doesn't stop here! Join us on our YouTube channel, Story Land Playground, where stories come to life with exciting read-alouds, engaging animations, and fun-filled learning adventures!

◆ **What You'll Find on Story Land Playground:**

✅ Read-Along Story Videos – Enjoy beautifully narrated read-alouds of your favorite books!

✅ Interactive Learning – Fun quizzes, educational videos, and exciting activities for kids!

✅ Music & Movement – Sing, dance, and learn with catchy songs and kid-friendly content!

✅ Confidence & Creativity Boosters – Fun challenges, storytelling tips, and writing activities to inspire young minds!

Perfect for Kids Ages 3-10, Parents, Teachers & Librarians!

📢 Visit us on YouTube today!

🎬 Watch the read-aloud version of this book and discover more amazing content!

SCAN ME

All of Our Books

COLOR ME COCO
COLORING BOOK

JOURNEY WITH COCO AND NAIYAH, A... COLOR THE WORLD!
AGES 3 +

Available at Walmart.com

Color Me Coco

MOM, CAN YOU TELL ME A STORY?
THE LOST LITTLE LION CUB

MY DAD THE SUPERHERO

A Tale of Two Chopsticks!
COCO & YURIKO

GO TO SLEEP LITTLE ONE

Available at BARNES & NOBLE

THE REAL EASTER STORY COLOURING BOOK!

Best Seller amazon.ca

GRANDMA'S HAN...
WRITTEN LATOYA...

Best Seller amazon.ca

I JUST LOVE CHRISTMAS
WRITTEN BY LATOYA A. BELFON

IZZY'S NEW LIFE
The Way I Talk
by Latoya Belfon

MUSICAL
ABC

Cadence
Learns Self-Love

Where Sleeps The Bear?

Where Flies The Bird?

Cadence Apprend à S'aimer Comme Il Est

Available at
amazon

www.ingramcontent.com/pod-product-compliance
Lightning Source LLC
Chambersburg PA
CBHW042108040426
42448CB00002B/185